TRIVIA WITH FUN FACTS ABOUT SAFARI ANIMALS

EXPLORE THE AFRICAN SAFARI ON TRIVIA NIGHT FOR ADULTS AND KIDS

CRITTER QUEST PUBLISHING

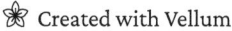 Created with Vellum

INTRODUCTION

Welcome to the captivating world of safari animals! This book is your ticket to an exciting animal safari, filled with mind-boggling trivia followed by fascinating facts. It will leave you amazed and excited to start your journey into the animal kingdom.

Imagine this: in the heart of the African wilderness, a young elephant calf gets separated from its herd during a thunderous storm. Lost and disoriented, the little elephant wanders through the dense underbrush, desperately searching for its family. Just as hope begins to fade, a seemingly unlikely savior emerges from the shadows.

A gentle giant with massive ears and wrinkled skin approaches the scared calf. It's a matriarchal herd of wild African buffalo. Instinctively recognizing the distress of their distant cousin, the buffalo encircle the vulnerable elephant, shielding it from predators and providing much-needed protection.

This heartwarming tale is just a glimpse into the remarkable and often unbelievable world of safari animals. Throughout this book, we'll explore the vast and diverse safari, from the graceful giraffes to the elusive leopards, from the playful meerkats to the majestic lions, the animal kingdom awaits you. Prepare to uncover bizarre and amazing facts about the animals you thought you knew so well. So, grab your binoculars, don your safari hat, and brace yourself for an unparalleled adventure that awaits!

Lions live together in groups of up to 25 lions, lionesses, and cubs. What is this group called?

A. Pack
B. Pride
C. Herd
D. Flock

The answer is B. Pride. This unique living situation makes them the most social of all the felines. A 'Pride' of lions usually comprises up to 80% females.

Which colorful, tiny bird is known for feeding on nectar like a hummingbird?

A. Collared Sunbird
B. Scarlet Macaw
C. Golden Pheasant
D. Violet-backed Starling

The answer is A. Collared Sunbird. This 2-3-inch-long bird loves to feed on nectar. It can hover like a hummingbird but will usually perch on a flower to eat. They have a green "collar" around their heads and upper body, giving them their name.

How much better can a Leopard see in the dark compared to a human?

A. 2 times better
B. 5 times better
C. 7 times better
D. 10 times better

The answer is C. 7 times better. Their adapted retinas will constrict or dilate according to the amount of light it needs, making them extraordinary nocturnal hunters. These solitary animals also have a tail as long as their bodies. It increases their balance and agility while running after their prey.

Which animal looks like a cow, feeds on fresh grass, but isn't related to them?

A. Buffalo
B. Wildebeest
C. Bison
D. Yak

The answer is A. Buffalo. These Herbivores can weigh up to 2,000 pounds and are not docile like cows. They are one of the most dangerous animals in the wild. Buffalo's are also very social. A 'Herd' of Buffalo can reach up to 1,000 Buffalo.

A cheetah is the fastest land animal and can reach a speed of what?

A. 60 miles per hour
B. 75 miles per hour
C. 90 miles per hour
D. 120 miles per hour

The answer is B. 75 miles per hour. Cheetahs can only hold this speed for a short time, so they get as close to their prey as they can and then sprint to catch it. They accelerate from 0-60 miles per hour in just 3 seconds.

What is the approximate size of an ostrich egg?

A. The size of a chicken egg
B. The size of a tennis ball
C. The size of a cantaloupe
D. The size of a football

The answer is C. The size of a cantaloupe. Ostrich eggs are the largest eggs on the planet. It can measure 6 inches in diameter and weigh up to 3 pounds. They usually lay, around seven eggs at a time and are put in a communal nest, which holds up to 60 eggs. So, when a chick emerges, it is already the size of a chicken.

Which tiny animal has a long and mobile nose, can jump 3 feet in the air, and can only be found in Africa?

A. Aardvark
B. Springhare
C. Dik-dik
D. Elephant Shrew

The answer is D. Elephant Shrew. These pocket-sized animals grow up to one foot in length and usually weigh less than a pound. Their nickname is the "Jumping Shrew" because they can run up to 18 miles per hour and jump 3 feet in the air. And they use their long, skinny tongues to feed on insects using their exceptional senses.

Vultures play a crucial role in nature by eating the carcasses of dead animals. What type of diet has helped them survive?

A. Herbivore
B. Scavenger
C. Omnivore
D. Carnivore

The answer is B. Scavenger. Vultures primarily feed on carrion, which is the leftover remains of a dead animal but will also follow and kill a wounded animal. In addition, they are known for "cleaning up" rotting carcasses left over by the predators, sometimes eating up to 20% of their body weight in one sitting. Some species will even consume the bones. Vultures have a specialized enzyme that neutralizes the bacteria known to be a danger to other animals. They have even been sighted eating side-by-side with other scavengers.

Which animal moves into abandoned aardvark dens?

A. Anteater
B. Wildebeest
C. Hyenas
D. Warthogs

The answer is D. Warthogs. The Warthog is an excellent digger but does not dig its own den. Instead, it moves into abandoned aardvark dens. They are native to Africa's east and southern regions and prefer cooler, open areas like savannahs and rain-forests.

Which of the following animals has a behavior where the males watch the young while the females forage for food?

A. Jackal
B. African Wild Dog
C. Meerkat
D. Bat-eared Fox

The answer is D. Bat-eared Fox. They are one of the few species where the males are the ones to watch the young while the females forage for food. The bat-eared fox eats primarily insects, but their favorite is the termite. They can consume up to 1.2 million termites a year.

What is the behavior exhibited by Leopard Tortoises when they feel threatened?

A. They run away as fast as they can.
B. They roll into a tight ball.
C. They tuck their head and feet inside their shell.
D. They hiss and bare their teeth.

The answer is C. They tuck their head and feet inside their shell. These animals are more defensive than offensive. When tucking their head and feet inside their shells, they squeeze the air from their lungs, often making a hissing sound. By doing this, they can commonly outwait the threat.

Which animal is known for its unique scales, long tongue and is the most trafficked mammal in the world?

A. Pangolin
B. Armadillo
C. Cheetah
D. Anteaters

The answer is A. Pangolin. They are the only scaled mammal on the planet. When faced with danger, they roll into a ball and use their scales as defensive armor. They also have no teeth in their mouths; instead, they have a long, mobile tongue they use to eat insects like ants and termites.

The aardvark is known for its ability to consume numerous ants and termites in a single night. Generally, how many ants and termites can an aardvark eat in one night?

A. 10,000
B. 20,000
C. 35,000
D. 50,000

The answer is D. 50,000. They use their long, sticky tongue, which can grow up to a foot, to reach inside the broken mound to harvest the ants and termites. Aardvarks eat these insects whole without chewing! Their stomach muscles break down the insects. To breach the rigid outer shell of these mounds, the aardvark uses its strong limbs and sharp claws. These prolific diggers can shift two feet of soil in 15 seconds.

Which bird holds the title of being the heaviest flying bird gifted with flight?

A. African Fish Eagle
B. Kori Bustard
C. Grey Crowned Crane
D. Southern Ground Hornbill

The answer is B. Kori Bustard. These grand birds can weigh up to 40 pounds and have a wingspan of up to 9 feet. These birds do not migrate, prefer the ground, and are opportunistic omnivores eating animals or plants.

Mountain gorillas are known for their highly social behavior and close bonds within their groups. Which of the following is true about their sleeping habits?

A. They sleep while hanging upside down from tree branches.
B. They sleep in underground burrows that they dig themselves.
C. They sleep in nests made from vegetation on the ground.
D. They sleep while perched on high tree branches.

The answer is C. They sleep in nests made from vegetation on the ground. They have nests in trees, but because of their weight, they have to ensure the tree supports them. Mountain gorillas have such a close bond; they like to snuggle while sleeping.

What color tongue does the tallest mammal in the world have?

A. Blue
B. Red
C. Pink
D. Green

The answer is A. Blue. A Giraffe has a blueish-purplish-blackish color tongue. The color helps protect the tongue from sunburn since they spend up to 18 hours a day looking for food and eat over 75 pounds of food a day. They use their 18-inch tongue to eat from the very top of trees. The acacia tree is a favorite to them.

What is the primary distinguishing feature between a white rhino and black rhino?

A. White rhinos are taller than black rhinos.
B. White rhinos have a hump on their back, while black rhinos have a straight back.
C. White rhinos have longer horns than black rhinos
D. White rhinos have a pointed lip, while black rhinos have a hooked lip.

The answer is D. White rhinos have a pointed lip, while black rhinos have a hooked lip. Also known for their thick skin, two horns on their snout, and three-toed hooves, these herbivores are the second largest land mammal. They are also the most ancient mammal found in Africa.

Which big cat is recognized for its exceptional adaptability and can flourish in various habitats?

A. Lion
B. Cheetah
C. Leopard
D. Tiger

The answer is C. Leopard. They have the broadest range of all the Big Cats. They are in the Far East, Northern, and Sub-Saharan Africa. You'll find a leopard in tropical rainforests, barren deserts, and mountain highlands, where there is good cover and ample food supply.

Which of the following is not true about the Secretary Bird?

A. It has been on an African postage stamp.
B. It is a bird of prey.
C. Its primary diet consists of fruits and seeds.
D. They only fly when necessary.

The answer is C. Its primary diet consists of fruits and seeds.
The Secretary Bird likes to hunt on foot. Some of their prey are insects, small mammals, snakes, bird eggs, and reptiles. They will use the thickened soles of their feet to stomp on their target, stunning it and then swallowing it whole.

How many months is the largest land mammal in the world pregnant?

A. 22 months
B. 17 months
C. 30 months
D. 26 months

The answer is A. 22 months. An elephant will give birth to a 3 feet tall, around 200-pound baby calf after 22 months. This calf will be protected by the herd of elephants, usually led by the matriarch.

Which antelope species can run up to 60 miles per hour and leap as far as 30 feet?

A. Springbok
B. Gemsbok
C. Wildebeest
D. Impala

The answer is D. Impala. It is one of the fastest and most common antelopes in Africa. Their numbers can reach up to 2 million. They use their powerful hind legs to leap as high as 10 feet and as far as 30 feet. They use this to go in different directions to confuse their predators.

How big are the ears of a bat-eared fox?

A. 7 cm
B. 9 cm
C. 13 cm
D. 15 cm

The answer is C. 13 cm. The ears of a bat-eared fox make up a third of its height. Their ability to hear insects underground gives them a powerful advantage over their predators. Hyenas, jackals, and eagles most threaten these nocturnal animals, but they are hard to catch.

Which of the following best describes the ant lion?

A. It is a fast runner.
B. It builds funnel-shaped pits to catch its prey.
C. It is a type of ant.
D. It feeds on nectar from flowers.

The answer is B. It builds funnel-shaped pits to catch its prey. The ant lion uses its abdomen to dig a 2-inch-deep hole to catch ants and other small insects.

"Pumba" means silly or foolish in Swahili. Which animal am I?

A. Zebra
B. Meerkat
C. Gazelle
D. Warthog

The answer is D. Warthog. These silly animals will forget that they are being chased by predators and stop because they forgot why they were running. On the end of their tails, they have "pom-poms," which they stick up while running. They do this so that other warthogs can follow them, but it's also easy for the predators to spot them.

Which facts about the honey badger are accurate?

A. They can dig a 10-foot-long tunnel in 10 minutes.
B. They are known as the most fearless animal on Earth, by the "Guinness Book of World Records"
C. They are like skunks and omit an odor from under their tails.
D. All the above

The answer is D. All the above. Honey badgers have sharp claws that can slice through a tortoise's shell. They use these claws to create the tunnel into hard Earth. They are the world's most fearless and ferocious animal. Honey Badgers have been known to steal a cub from a cheetah's den.

A 'mob' of meerkats can have up to how many members?

A. 25 members
B. 40 members
C. 50 members
D. 65 members

The answer is C. 50 members. Most families have 20 members, but a few 'super-families' exist. These omnivores work together to build, burrow, protect, and find food. They have exceptional eyesight that helps them see a bird in the sky. They are also immune to venom and know how to eat scorpions and millipedes.

What tiny bird eats ticks off a Rhino, Buffalo, and Hippo?

A. Oxpecker
B. Finch
C. Hummingbird
D. Sparrow

The answer is A. Oxpecker. An oxpecker can eat hundreds of ticks and over 12,000 larvae off these giant mammals. They use their sharp claws to cling to the surfaces of these animals, where they sleep, eat, and interact with each other. These birds have also been known to produce a loud shrilling call to alert their host when they notice potential danger.

Which predatory insect has a pouncing behavior reminiscent of a lion?

A. Ant Lion
B. Praying Mantis
C. Lady Bug
D. Butterfly

The answer is A. Ant Lion. The ant lion was observed by early scholars who saw it "pounce" like a lion, giving it its name. In addition, the ant lion catches prey of ants and other small insects.

The jackass penguin earned its unique name how?

A. Its long, protruding beak resembles a donkey's snout.
B. It's braying call that mirrors a donkey.
C. It's hardworking and loyal to its mate, like a donkey.
D. Its distinctive black and white coat pattern similar to a donkey

The answer is B. It's braying call that mirrors a donkey. They use this loud braying call to communicate with each other while they are defending themselves. This flightless, 2 feet tall bird will also bend down to fight its attacker using its beak. They can also swim up to 12 miles per hour and stay underwater for over 2 minutes.

Which animal has the closest DNA to humans?

A. Chimpanzee
B. Gorilla
C. Bonobo
D. Orangutan

The answer is A. Chimpanzee. Chimpanzees share up to 98% of the same DNA as humans. Therefore, they are more closely related to a human than a gorilla. Sadly, that means they are also susceptible to human diseases.

Which cat is the strongest in Africa and can drag a heavier animal up a tree?

A. Cheetah
B. Lion
C. African wildcat
D. Leopard

The answer is D. Leopard. They are known for their strength, agility, climbing abilities, and navigation. They use their powerful hind legs to propel them forward while having a long, sturdy tail to keep them centered. With their retractable claws, they grip the bark of a tree, enabling them to hoist their prey high up in the branches. This strategy allows them to eat their meal away from potential predators safely.

How do warthogs position themselves while feeding?

A. Standing upright
B. Sitting on their hind legs
C. Laying on their backs
D. Lowering to the ground and resting on their forearms

The answer is D. Lowering to the ground and resting on their forearms. They are omnivores but favor grass and tubers. When food is scarce, they will scavenge carcasses and eat insects but not hunt. They can also go months without water.

What is the predominant feature of the Lilac-breasted Roller?

A. Large crest on its head
B. Vibrant blue plumage
C. Long, curved beak
D. Elongated tail feathers

The answer is B. Vibrant blue plumage. This colorful bird is the national bird of Kenya. Its wing feathers are a mix of purple and blue, while the body has turquoise and lilac. The head has a green crown with cream around the eyes, and the back has brown feathers. It perches at the tops of trees to swoop in on larger prey, like lizards, scorpions, small birds, and rodents.

How do giraffes typically sleep?

A. Standing up
B. Lying down on their sides
C. Hanging from tree branches
D. Burrowing in the ground

The answer is A. Standing up. Giraffes sleep standing up with their necks and heads resting on their bodies or tree branches. This unique way of sleeping allows them to react quickly to potential danger. They have also adapted to only needing around 2 hours of sleep.

Which kingfisher species is capable of sustaining hovering flight?

A. Malachite Kingfisher
B. Brown-hooded Kingfisher
C. Pled Kingfisher
D. African Pygmy Kingfisher

The answer is C. Pled Kingfisher. This bird has a unique ability to sustain hovering flight while trying to catch fish, while most kingfishers will perch and then dive in. This ability, along with their keen eyesight, allows them to target and then descend to get their meal accurately.

What is another name for the Rhinoceros Beetle?

A. Titan Beetle
B. Hercules Beetle
C. Goliath Beetle
D. Atlas Beetle

The answer is B. Hercules Beetle. Being able to lift up to 850 times its body weight, this beetle is among the largest in the world. Also, the Rhinoceros beetle is named for its horned feature on male heads.

This gentle giant's saying is more truth than fiction.

A. Elephants - "Elephants never forget."
B. Sperm Whale - "Sperm whales sing the loudest songs."
C. Giant Panda - "Giant pandas are always peaceful."
D. Rhinoceros - "A Rhino never forgets the comfort of home."

The answer is A. Elephants - "Elephants never forget." They will remember an encounter they had in passing and can always find alternate routes to food and water when a dry spell occurs. Additionally, they have also been known to have empathy and will dig a hole and bury a loved one when they pass.

Which of the following statements is true about mountain gorillas?

A. They give birth once a year.
B. They are solitary animals.
C. They are the second-largest primate in the world.
D. They are not endangered.

The answer is C. They are the second-largest primate in the world. These powerful primates can weigh between 400 and 500 pounds. And they are as tall as a human, 4-6 feet tall when standing. They are one of the most powerful primates on the planet and live in Central Africa high up in the mountains at an altitude between 8,000-13,000 feet.

Which small mammal, often mistaken for a rodent, is known as the "rock rabbit" and has specialized feet to help them on rocky surfaces?

A. African Hedgehog
B. Rock Python
C. Rock Hyrax
D. Cape Ground Squirrel

The answer is C. Rock Hyrax. "Rock Dassie" is also another name for the Rock Hyrax. Rock Hyraxes aren't actually related to rodents but to Elephants and Manatees. Their specialized feet, which are rubber soles indented in the middle to create a suction-like effect, help them navigate dangerous ledges and slippery rocks.

Which statement is true about the hippo?

A. It is the most deadly mammal in the world
B. It is the loudest mammal in the world.
C. It is the third-largest living land mammal.
D. All of the above

The answer is D. All of the above. These massive animals can weigh up to 4,400 pounds and measure up to 16 feet in length. A Hippo's wheezes/snorts can be heard a mile away, and it was even recorded that their sounds could reach up to 115 decibels, which is the volume of loud, close thunder. Hippos are known to be aggressive animals, and being big with powerful jaws makes them one of the deadliest mammals.

How many white lions are believed to be in existence today?

A. Around 13
B. Around 37
C. Around 52
D. Around 79

The answer is A. Around 13. These rare lions have a recessive gene that causes the white skin coloring. They are still being born in Nature Reserves, which proves that white lions are a natural occurrence.

Which omnivore is closely related to the fox, looks like a fox, and has one mate for life?

A. Raccoon
B. African wild dog
C. Hyena
D. Jackal

The answer is D. Jackal. The jackal and foxes are close relatives with similar-looking bodies and bushy tails. Jackals have one mate for life and will communicate with unique sounds, so only their tribe will get the message.

What is the purpose of a flamingo's unique beak shape?

A. It helps them catch fish underwater.
B. It allows them to filter-feed on tiny organisms.
C. It serves as a weapon for defense.
D. It aids in regulating their temperature.

The answer is B. It allows them to filter-feed on tiny organisms. Their unique beak curves downward, so when they turn their head upside-down in the water, they can filter out tiny organisms like algae, shrimp, and snails. Eating this type of diet causes the feathers to turn pink. Therefore, when a flamingo is born, it is born white. It takes about two years for them to turn pink.

Which of these characteristics is true about the very rare nocturnal Bush Baby?

A. They have excellent hearing.
B. They can see in the dark
C. Their cry is similar to a human baby.
D. All of the above

The answer is D. All of the above. They can hear insects flying with their large ears and also fold their ears against their heads to block out any noise when they sleep. Their huge eyes allow them to see in the dark to pursue their prey. And they are very vocal animals, signaling to each other when danger is near.

Which exciting fact about the lion is not true?

A. Its roar is the loudest of all the cats.
B. The males hunt for the food
C. They spend about 20 hours a day resting.
D. They can consume as much as 15% of their body weight.

The answer is B. The males hunt for the food. Lionesses hunt for prey while the males get to eat first, followed by the cubs, then the lionesses. They are the top carnivore of the safari, and their roars can be witnessed up to 5 miles away.

This 'Architect of the bird world' bird builds elaborate nests using grass and twigs. Which bird am I?

A. Buffalo Weaver
B. Hornbill
C. Weaver Finch
D. Sparrow

The answer is A. Buffalo Weaver. They are known for constructing communal nests with separate rooms. Multiple pairs contribute to these nests that provide them shelter and protection from predators and unfavorable weather conditions.

Which animal is the lion's #1 threat?

A. Hyena
B. Buffalo
C. Crocodile
D. Leopard

The answer is B. Buffalo. These aggressive animals are considered dangerous. They have a heavy shield across their forehead that leads to large horns. These horns can have a horizontal spread of 3 feet with a length and around 5 feet along the curve.

The elephant's trunk is the planet's most versatile and helpful appendage. So, how many muscles does it contain?

A. 10,000 muscles
B. 25,000 muscles
C. 40,000 muscles
D. 55,000 muscles

The answer is C. 40,000 muscles. The trunk has 40,000 muscles divided into as many as 150,000 parts. Elephants use their trunk to gather food, drink water, handle objects, pick up scents, take dust baths, comfort the young, communicate, and so much more.

How does the little bee-eater catch and eat its food?

A. It swoops down from a perch to catch insects in mid-air
B. It uses its long tongue to extract nectar from flowers
C. It digs into the ground to find worms and larvae
D. It scavenges for small vertebrates like lizards and frogs

The answer is A. It swoops down from a perch to catch insects in midair. It will patiently wait till it sees an insect, especially a bee, wasp, or hornet, then swoop in to catch it. Then, it removes the stinger by repeatedly hitting the bee on a hard surface before it eats it.

Which of these facts about the marabou stork are true?

A. It is considered one of the world's ugliest birds.
B. It eats carrion, scraps, and feces.
C. It has a large, bare head with a long, wrinkled neck.
D. All of the above

The answer is D. All of the above. The marabou stork is unmistakable due to its stature and appearance. Its head has adapted to being bare because it sticks its whole head inside the corpse when it eats. As a result, the feathers on the top of its head would come out matted with blood. This large bird also has hollow leg and toe bones to help reduce its weight when it flies.

The International Union for Conservation of Nature (IUCN) classifies the cheetah as vulnerable. So, what is their estimated population in the wild now?

A. 5,000
B. 6,000
C. 7,000
D. 8,000

The answer is C. 7,000. There is a growing number of cheetahs in zoos, but habitat loss and an increase in natural parks are decreasing the numbers in the wild. So, the total left in the world is about 8,500 cheetahs.

Which animal is part of the order Tubulidentata, a specific prehistoric mammal species?

A. Pangolin
B. Rhinoceros
C. Aardvark
D. Elephant

The answer is C. Aardvark. They are the only living species from this prehistoric order from 2 million years ago. Being from this order, came its most unique feature: its teeth. Unlike most mammals, an aardvark's tooth comprises up to 1,500 straw-like tubes, constantly replacing and regrowing.

How long can a giraffe, the tallest mammal in the world, go without drinking water?

A. Up to 1 weeks
B. Up to 2 weeks
C. Up to 3 weeks
D. Up to 4 weeks

The answer is C. Up to 3 weeks. A giraffe gets most of its water from the 75 pounds of leaves it eats daily. When it notices water, it awkwardly spreads its front legs to get its head low enough to the ground to drink. They must do this because their necks are too short and their hind legs too long.

What is Africa's top wildlife experience?

A. Safari game drives in the Serengeti
B. Gorilla trekking in the Virunga Mountains
C. Hot air balloon safari over the Masai Mara
D. Witnessing the wildebeest migration in the Serengeti

The answer is D. Witnessing the wildebeest migration in the Serengeti. Between May and June, up to 2 million Wildebeest, zebras, and other grazers migrate north to lusher pastures. This incredible operation is an awe-inspiring event that shows Africa's power, beauty, and resilience.

Which animal has a big mouth and can walk underwater in its sleep?

A. Crocodile
B. Seal
C. Dolphin
D. Hippopotamus

The answer is D. Hippopotamus. They can stretch their jaws 150 degrees. They do this to show dominance and threaten any predators. When open, the hippo's mouth can stretch up to 4 feet tall, and its bite is about 100 times stronger than a human's. Hippos can't swim but walk along the bottom of waterways. They can hold their breaths for up to 5 minutes before resurfacing. This action comes so naturally to them that they can walk underwater in their sleep.

The honey badger's skin is impressive in many ways, but there is one thing it cannot do. What is it?

A. Protect against venomous bites.
B. Prevent injuries from sharp objects.
C. Repel Water
D. Withstand extreme temperatures.

The answer is C. Repel Water. Honey badgers have steel-like skin that protects them against venom when preying on black mambas, scorpions, and porcupines. And as their name suggests, they love honey and will snatch the entire beehive to get to it. Plus, the bee stings don't affect them at all.

The rock hyrax has a unique digestive system that aids in breaking down the plants it consumes. What is the primary function of the bacteria in its three-chambered stomach?

A. Producing venom to aid in digestion.
B. Absorbing water to prevent dehydration.
C. Breaking down the leaves and grass into digestible compounds
D. Secreting enzymes for protein digestion

The answer is C. Breaking down the leaves and grass into digestible compounds. The rock hyrax's three-chambered stomach produces bacterium to help break down food, but their babies aren't born with it. The babies need to eat the poop from the adults to get the bacteria it needs for digestion.

Which hyena species is known for its distinctive laughing vocalization?

A. Spotted Hyena
B. Striped Hyena
C. Brown Hyena
D. Aardwolf

The answer is A. Spotted Hyena. This laughing vocalization is a unique characteristic of only the spotted hyena. It is used to communicate with their clan members, and the pitch of their laugh also reveals its age.

A porcupine uses its spiny quills on its back and tail against which natural predator?

A. Lion
B. Eagle
C. Snake
D. Fish

The answer is A. Lion. A few other natural predators are the great horned owl, black bear, bobcat, and coyote. When a predator approaches, it turns its back to them and always keeps its 30,000 quills facing a threat.

One of these facts is not true about the zebra. Which one is it?

A. A group of zebras is called a "Dazzle."
B. Zebras are white with black stripes.
C. They can outrun a lion.
D. Their stripes are unique, like a human fingerprint.

The answer is B. Zebras are white with black stripes. They are actually black with white stripes. They can also rotate their ears in almost any direction to help them hear when a predator approaches. Then they flee in a zigzag pattern up to 40 miles per hour, making it difficult for the predator to catch them.

Which bird is known for its striking appearance with a crown of golden feathers on its head?

A. Ostrich
B. Grey Crowned Crane
C. African Penguin
D. Scarlet Macaw

The answer is B. Grey Crowned Crane. This bird is known for its distinctive crown of stiff golden feathers on the top of its head. The grey-crowned crane has been the national bird of Uganda for more than 100 years. It symbolizes elegance and beauty to them.

Which statement is not true about the African wild dog?

A. They are the world's most friendly dogs and do everything as a group
B. They have long, round ears and beautiful fur
C. They start eating their prey while it's still alive
D. They have 5 toes on each foot, making them fast

The answer is D. They have 5 toes on each foot, making them fast. Unlike most canines, the African wild dog only has four toes on its forefeet versus five. It expands their stride and increases their speed. So even though they are not the fastest, they have greater stamina. That perseverance makes them successful at obtaining their prey.

This reptile is the largest in Africa, the second-largest in the world, and has a bite five times stronger than a lion. Who am I?

A. Anaconda
B. Nile Crocodile
C. Black Mamba
D. Komodo Dragon

The answer is B. Nile Crocodile. This crocodile can grow up to 20 feet long and weigh between 500 and 1,650 pounds. These crocodiles have no natural predators due to their exceptional ability to camouflage and formidable hunting skills.

Which antelope is the largest and slowest, known for its impressive size and distinctive spiral horns?

A. Eland
B. Kudu
C. Roan
D. Hartebeest

The answer is A. Eland. These giants can reach a height of 9.5 feet and a length of 9 feet and weigh over 2,000 pounds. In addition, they have 12 stripes on their body to help with camouflage and a tight spiral horn; a female's horns can be larger than a male's at 27 inches. These non-aggressive animals adapt to many African areas as long as there is plenty of food; leaves from flowering plants are a favorite.

What is a distinctive feature of the southern masked weaver bird?

A. Ability to mimic other bird calls.
B. Long migratory flights
C. Intricate nest-building skills
D. Exceptional diving abilities

The answer is C. Intricate nest-building skills. The southern masked weaver can build up to 25 nests per breeding season. They use reeds and grass to build their nests, which are suspended over water and can reach a height of 10 feet. These birds can also hang upside-down using their talons to build their nests.

How many teeth does a Nile crocodile go through in their lifetime?

A. 2,500 teeth
B. 2,000 teeth
C. 1,500 teeth
D. 1,000 teeth

The answer is B. 2,000 teeth. When a tooth gets lost or damaged, a new tooth comes in, and it will last around two years. So, this predator, who has no natural enemies, has between 64-68 cone-shaped teeth.

Which fact about the Aardwolf is accurate?

A. It is a member of the hyena family.
B. It can eat around a quarter of a million termites in one night.
C. They are territorial and raise their manes in warning.
D. All the above

The answer is D. All the above. They are the only members of the hyena family not to devour carrion or hunt large animals. Their mouth and teeth have adapted to their eating habits. They use their long sticky tongue to lick termites right off the ground.

A group of porcupines is called what?

A. Quill
B. Bundle
C. Prickle
D. Cluster

The answer is C. Prickle. A 'prickle' of porcupines will primarily gather together during the winter. Other than that, they are solitary herbivores. Also, these rodents are the third largest in the world, eating up to a pound of food a day.

Which fact is not true about the ostrich.

A. They are the tallest flightless bird.
B. They are the heaviest flightless bird.
C. They are the fastest land runners.
D. They have the largest eyes of any known land animal in the world.

The answer is C. They are the fastest land runners. The cheetah is faster than an ostrich, but an ostrich can run up to 45 miles per hour and is said to be the quickest runner among birds. To help with this speed, they only have two toes versus three toes, like all other birds. Also, their eyes are 2 inches across, making them five times bigger than a human's. It lets them see a lot farther to protect them. For example, they can see an object the size of a big dog a mile and a half away.

Chimpanzees are known for their remarkable intelligence and communication skills. Which of the following is true about their communication?

A. They communicate using a complex system of clicks and whistles.
B. They use sign language to communicate with humans.
C. They have the ability to understand and use different vocalizations.
D. They communicate through a series of dance-like movements.

The answer is C. They have the ability to understand and use different vocalizations. They have been known to have up to 30 distinct calls, which can be heard as far away as a mile and a half. However, even with this ability, they prefer using facial expressions and communicating through physical touch. As one of the most intelligent animal species, the chimpanzee enjoys embracing, kissing, patting each other on the back, and touching while playing.

AFTERWORD

Exploring this world of safari animals has been an exciting journey filled with intriguing trivia with fun facts. We burrowed into the magnificent creatures that roam the African Savannah, from the mighty lions and buffalo to the tiny rhinoceros beetles and oxpeckers. Throughout this book, you have learned about their intricate social structures, impressive hunting techniques, and astonishing survival strategies in Africa's challenging environment.

As we conclude this trivia and fun fact book, let us reflect on the diversity and beauty of safari animals. Through their extraordinary stories and abilities, they remind us of the awe-inspiring wonders that exist in the animal kingdom. Therefore, let us continue to appreciate and protect these magnificent creatures with a deeper understanding of their intricate web of life. Furthermore, let us ensure that future generations can also marvel at the wonders of the African safari.

LEAVE A REVIEW!

We would be incredibly grateful if you could take just 60 seconds to support us and write a brief review on Amazon.

RESOURCES

Adventure Travel & Nature Tours | Natural Habitat Adventures. (n.d.). https://www.nathab.com/

Agent. (2021, November 15). *Wildlife - Lion, Leopards, Cheetah, Elephant - African Wildlife Safaris.* African Wildlife Safaris. https://africanwildlifesafaris.com/wildlife

AZ Animals. (2023, April 23). *Animal Encyclopedia With Facts, Pictures, Definitions, and More! - AZ Animals.* https://a-z-animals.com/

Beach, S. (2018). Interesting Safari Trivia Facts. *Safari and Beach.* https://safariandbeach.com/interesting-safari-trivia-facts/

Garside, V. (2022). 50+ African Safari Animals (Facts, Pics + Where to Find Them!). *MakeTimeToSeeTheWorld.* https://maketimetoseetheworld.com/big-five-african-safari-animals/

Kings Camp Blog | Kings Camp Private Game Reserve. (2019, April 9). Kings Camp. https://kingscamp.com/blog

Magazine, S. (2023, May 19). *History, Travel, Arts, Science, People, Places Smithsonian Magazine.* https://www.smithsonianmag.com/

Printed in Dunstable, United Kingdom